W9-CRZ-558

DELiCiOUS CHiCKEN SOUP

LIBRARY EDITION

RECIPE BY CHEF ANDREY DURBACH
GHOST WRITTEN BY ROBERT CHAPLiN *rca bfa*

© AD MMViii Durbach and Chaplin, all rights reserved.
Published in Canada by Robert Chaplin *rca bfa*.
Library and Archives Canada Cataloguing in Publication
Durbach, Andrey, 1967– Delicious chicken soup/Andrey Durbach;
illustrator: Robert Chaplin. – Library ed. isbn 978-1-894897-90-7

1. Delicious Soups. 2. Cookery (Chicken). I. Chaplin, Rob, 1968– II. Title.

TX757.D87 2008   641.8'13   C2008-906645-6

PRINTED AT FRIESENS IN CANADA. FABRiQUE AU CANADA.

MAKiNG DELiCiOUS CHiCKEN SOUP iS AN ART, WHiCH PROViDES COMFORT AND GOOD FEELiNGS TO EVERYONE WE KNOW, FROM THE YOUNGEST CHiLD TO THE OLDEST MiCHELiN CHEF.[iii]

FiRST YOU WiLL NEED TO GET STUFF TO COOK WiTH, TOOLS AND iNGREDiENTS.

TOOLS

A STOVE

A BiG POT

A SHARP KNiFE

A CUTTiNG BOARD

A STRAiNER

A LADLE

A BiG BOWL

A COOKiE SHEET

BOWLS AND SPOONS

A VEGETABLE PEELER

AN OLD TiN CAN *

* see substitutions

iNGREDiENTS

1 CHiCKEN 2½ - 3 lbs

1 BiG ONiON

2 BiG CARROTS

2 BiG CELERY RiBS

optional additions

1 TURNiP

1 LEEK

necessary herbs and spices

SALT............3 tablespoons

PEPPER.......1 teaspoon

2 BAY LEAVES

FRESH THYME 5 sprigs

A LiTTLE PiECE of GiNGER

(adult thumb sized)

NEXT YOU HAVE TO PREPARE AND MEASURE YOUR iNGREDiENTS

PEEL
THE CARROTS
THEN CUT THEM
iN HALF
PEEL
THE ONiON
CUT iN FOUR
PEEL
THE TURNiP
CUT iN FOUR
SPLiT
AND WASH
THE LEEK
WASH
THE CELERY
CUT iN HALF
RiNSE
THE CHiCKEN
iNSiDE AND OUT
(but not inside out!)

Now you can begin to make delicious chicken soup, this part happens rather quickly.

spring chicken with spring flowers

PUT YOUR iNGREDiENTS iN THE POT

put the carrots in the pot
put the celery in the pot
put the onions in the pot
put the turnips in the pot
put the leeks into the pot
put the chicken in the pot

PUT THE HERBS AND SPiCES iN THE POT

put the ginger in the pot

put the thyme into the pot

put the bay leaf in the pot

put the salt into the pot

put the pepper in the pot

put cold water in the pot

* make sure to use enough water to well cover all of your ingredients.

USE COLD WATER!

COLD WATER CONTAINS MORE OXYGEN.

and oxygen adds flavour to liquids and helps to make your soup taste delicious.

THEN
put the pot on the stove, on a burner, and turn it up to hot.
AS HOT AS iT WiLL GO!

HOT
HOT
HOT

Bring the pot to a BOiL

A boil is when your pot is bubbling. In a rapid boil there are lots and lots of bubbles in the pot the pot is bubbling a lot. Keep your eye on the pot. As the pot comes to a boil watch for the scummy foam which rises to the top.

Then, turn the heat down
and use your ladle to skim off the
scummy foam, periodically, until it is
all gone. Put the scummy foam into

THE
OLD
TiN
CAN

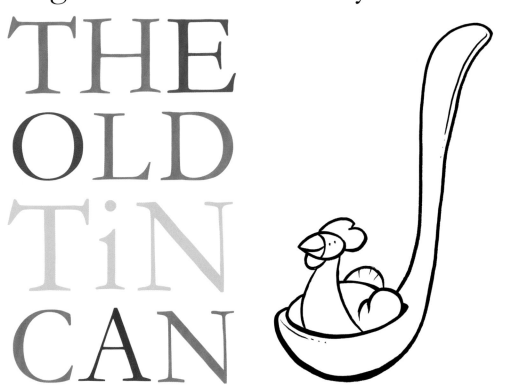

It is important to skim off the scummy foam, so that we may have a CLEAR CLEAN SOUP

✳ Convection, from boiling water, will drive the scummy foam down into the soup. This is why it is important to turn the heat down. This part happens rather slowly, so take your time, skim off the foam. Convection is the transference of mass or heat within a fluid, caused by the tendency of warmer and less dense material to rise.

Let your soup simmer

a simmer is a very slow boil, there are only a few bubbles, and the bubbles are slow. Let your soup simmer for approximately two whole hours.

THEN, TURN THE STOVE OFF.

Let everything cool down, you can tidy up your kitchen and then go away, for approximately two whole hours.

spring chicken in late winter

when you come back THE CHiCKEN FAT will be at the top of the soup. Use your ladle to skim off THE CHiCKEN FAT and then put the chicken fat into...

THE
OLD
TiN
CAN

(see iv. matzo balls)

Now, carefully pour your soup through your strainer into the large bowl. Pick out the chicken and vegetables and place them on the cookie sheet. Discard the old herbs, put the bay leaves, the thyme sprigs, and the little piece of ginger into

THE
OLD
TiN
CAN

The vegetables and the chicken ought to be cool enough to handle. Use your cutting board and knife to cut the vegetables into bite sized pieces: cut the carrots into coins, cut the celery into sickle moons, cut the turnip into little turnip pieces, cut the onion into little onion pieces, cut the leek into little leek pieces… Put the cut up vegetables back into the pot.

chicken under sickle moon

Use your fingers to separate the chicken meat from the chicken skin and bones. Cut the chicken meat into bite-sized pieces. Put the bite-sized chicken meat pieces back into the pot. Put the chicken skin and bones into

THE
OLD
TiN
CAN

Put the pot with the soup, cut up vegetables, and chicken meat back on the stove. Then turn up the heat, not super hot, bring to a medium simmer. Then taste your soup. (think about it)  $\approx \infty$ ask yourself, "is there enough salt?" If there is enough, leave it alone. If you need a little more salt then add a little more salt. Your delicious chicken soup is complete. It is ready to eat.

* see variations and additions. At this point you may want to add other ingredients to your delicious chicken soup, like noodles, peas, fresh chopped parsley, black truffles, matzo balls. The possibilities are unlimited.

OTHERWiSE USE BOWLS AND SPOONS TO SERVE AND ENjOY

You may
throw out
THE
OLD
TiN
CAN

TO PERFECT OUR DELiCiOUS CHiCKEN SOUP, WE MUST ACTUALLY MAKE iT. A RECiPE iS NOT A SOUP, A RECiPE iS A WORKiNG DOCUMENT. AND THAT iS SOMETHiNG EVERYONE MUST KNOW FROM THE YOUNGEST CHiLD TO THE OLDEST MiCHELiN CHEF. PERFECTiON COMES THROUGH TRiAL, REPETiTiON, AND REFiNEMENT. MEANiNG THAT, THROUGH YOUR EXPERiENCE, YOU MAY WANT TO ALTER THE RECiPE iN SUBTLE WAYS.

THE END

APPENDICES

i. practical, not precise, conversions

ONE TEASPOON EQUALS 5 ML

ONE TABLESPOON EQUALS 15 ML

ONE FLUID OUNCE EQUALS 30 ML

ONE CUP EQUALS 250 ML

ONE PINT (2 CUPS) EQUALS 500 ML

ONE QUART (4 CUPS) EQUALS 1 LITER

ONE GALLON (4 QUARTS) EQUALS 4 LITERS

ONE OUNCE EQUALS 25 GRAMS

ONE POUND (lb) EQUALS 450 GRAMS

A PINCH IS A PINCH A DASH IS TWO PINCHES
A DROP IS A DROP SIX DROPS IS A DASH
AND A JIGGER'S AN OUNCE AND A HALF.

ii. substitutions

Things you can use instead of

THE OLD TiN CAN

an empty milk carton or a garbage can.

iii. Michelin Chef

To be a Michelin chef, one has to be in charge of the kitchen when a restaurant is awarded one or more Michelin stars.

In 1900, André Michelin published the first edition of a guide to France; to help drivers maintain their cars, find decent lodging, and eat well while touring. The Michelin Guide (Le Guide Michelin) is a series of annual guide books, published by Michelin, for over a dozen countries. The term refers by default to the Michelin Red Guide, the oldest and best-known European hotel and restaurant guide, which awards the Michelin stars. †
Michelin stars are awarded to restaurants offering the finest cooking, regardless of cuisine style. Stars represent only what is on the plate. They do not take into consideration interior decoration, service quality or table settings. ††

❀ *a very good restaurant in its category*
❀❀ *excellent cooking worth a detour*
❀❀❀ *exceptional cuisine worth the journey*

† wikipedia.org
†† michelinguide.com

iv. VARiATiONS AND ADDiTiONS

SOUP FROM BONES

SUBSTiTUTE THREE POUNDS (lbs) CHICKEN BONES FOR WHOLE CHICKEN. USE UNCOOKED BONES! iT iS POiNTLESS TO TRY TO MAKE DELiCiOUS CHiCKEN SOUP FROM THE BONES OF AN ALREADY COOKED CHiCKEN.

CHiCKEN NOODLE SOUP

ADD YOUR FAVORiTE STYLE OF NOODLES AT THE APPROPRiATE TiME

MATZO BALLS

2 TABLESPOONS OF MELTED CHiCKEN FAT OR OLiVE OiL
2 EGGS BEATEN
1/2 CUP OF MATZO MEAL
1 TEASPOON SALT
2 TABLESPOONS WATER
1/8 TEASPOON NUTMEG
1/2 TEASPOON GROUND BLACK PEPPER

MIX THE FAT AND EGGS TOGETHER IN A BOWL, THEN ADD THE MATZO MEAL, SALT, PEPPER, AND NUTMEG. MIX TOGETHER, UNTIL WELL BLENDED, THEN ADD THE WATER. COVER THE BOWL AND REFRIGERATE FOR AT LEAST 20 MINUTES. TAKE THE MIXTURE OUT OF THE FRIDGE. WET YOUR HANDS, AND THEN USE YOUR HANDS TO FORM GOLF BALL SIZED BALLS WITH THE MIXTURE. DROP THE BALLS INTO GENTLY SIMMERING, SALTED, WATER. COVER THE POT AND LET COOK FOR 30-40 MINUTES, UNTIL TENDER. SCOOP THE MATZO BALLS OUT OF THE POT WITH A SLOTTED SPOON, AND PLACE DIRECTLY INTO YOUR BOWL OF DELICIOUS CHICKEN SOUP.

TiNY DUMPLiNGS

2 LARGE EGGS BEATEN
1/2 CUP MiLK
1 1/4 CUPS ALL PURPOSE FLOUR
1/4 TEASPOON SALT
1/2 TEASPOON BAKING POWDER
1/8 TEASPOON GROUND NUTMEG
1/2 BUNCH CHOPPED PARSLEY
2 TABLESPOONS OF OiL
FOR OiLING THE COLANDER

MIX ALL OF THE INGREDIENTS TOGETHER, BLEND UNTIL SMOOTH, USE AN ELECTRIC BEATER OR WHISK BY HAND. OIL UP THE COLANDER AND PLACE OVER A LARGE POT OF BOILING WATER. SPOON HALF THE MIXTURE INTO THE COLANDER. THEN USE THE BACK OF YOUR SPOON TO PRESS THE MIXTURE THROUGH THE HOLES IN THE COLANDER, INTO THE WATER. WAIT FOR THE TINY DUMPLINGS TO FLOAT TO THE TOP OF THE POT (ABOUT ONE MINUTE). THEY ARE DONE! SCOOP THE TINY DUMPLINGS OUT OF THE WATER AND PUT THEM INTO YOUR DELiCiOUS CHiCKEN SOUP POT AND REPEAT.